D1564304

BASIC DISASTER SUPPLIES KIT

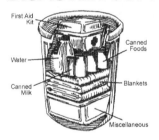

First Aid Kit

Water

Canned Milk

Canned Foods

Blankets

Miscellaneous

BASIC DISASTER SUPPLIES KIT

poems

Marci Rae Johnson

STEEL TOE BOOKS BOWLING GREEN, KENTUCKY

Copyright © 2015 Marci Rae Johnson

ALL RIGHTS RESERVED
PRINTED IN THE UNITED STATES

ISBN: 978-0-9863575-1-0

STEEL TOE BOOKS
Western Kentucky University
Department of English
1906 College Heights Blvd. #11086
Bowling Green, Kent. 42101-1086

BOOK DESIGNED BY THOM CARAWAY
COVER ART BY ELIZABETH WUERFFEL

Steel Toe Books is affiliated with Western Kentucky University

Contents

i.

ii.

iii.

i.

MR. ROGERS IS FLIPPING YOU OFF

Mr. Rogers puts his pants on one leg
at a time like everyone else. On TV
he's already wearing pants. He dons
his shoes and sweater as if he's about
to leave for work, but his work is to stay
and play with puppets and the train set
your father gave you last year and hasn't
had time to set up. Mr. Rogers is using
his degree in music composition to teach
you how to count. He counts the middle
finger of his right hand without irony like
your father in church, pointing to the Bible
verse he wants you to memorize. You
comply, though your understanding's hazy,
the caption on your drawing: "do not
comet adultery." The man and woman
in the movie today about the end
of the world have managed not to love
each other until now. Icy bodies hurtling
to earth and they are running out of time.
Never enough time to love and be loved.

WE WANT A GOD WHO FEELS LONELY

It is bad that I am alone. I should have someone to talk to.
"Old Man Coyote Makes the World"

Man must have a woman Because it is not good for him to
be alone Because he needs someone to help him name the
owl with the particular voice Because he is bored Because
nothing is fun anymore Because he can't remember the punch
line of that dumb joke from the TV show Because there
aren't any children There are only the hard shells of insects
and the swords that were left behind when the last person
surrendered and the fires were put out and the soft skin of the
sand became rough where the trees disappeared and there
was nothing to shade them and there was nowhere to stand
and say hallelujah or I love you or who left the toilet seat up
again. It is bad that there is only water and nothing else That
the earth is formless that God is only a spirit and not a man
who walks in the yard away from the pile of wood from the
unfinished project in the garage. It is not good for him to feel
the empty space in the bed where her feet were cold and he
would make them warm again.

APOPHENIA

The experience of seeing meaningful patterns or
connections in random or meaningless data.
Wikipedia

After she had taken the toast from the toaster,
trimmed the crusts and spread the butter just so.

After she had sprinkled the cinnamon
and the sugar. After she had poured the juice

into the thick glass from the wedding, opaqued
by the dishwasher's heat, she sat with her back

to the window and watched him eat without
tasting, the TV in the background yelling

the scores from last night's game over and over
so she would never forget. She watched him chew,

his cheeks bulging, and thought of last night's
pastoral visit from her lover: in her sleep his eyes

closed above her, his prayer that she would keep.
The toast on the plate half eaten was

the forgotten face of Jesus: a miracle, the juice
turning red with the sun rising outside the window.

APPARATUS FOR FACILITATING THE BIRTH OF A CHILD BY CENTRIFUGAL FORCE

US patent #3216423

When a woman is ready
she lies on her back. The mechanism
is complex, the acts

in unison. She may be hot
to the touch, her mouth open
to the alien light.

Though her hands may reach out
across her body
she must be properly directed.

When a woman is ready
she must be strapped down,
the blue dressing gown

half-shocked across the shoulder.
The movement must remind her
of the night on the ballroom floor

the spin and the swerve, and after,
the bed of coats from the guests
where you pushed her into

the fur and the flame, kissed her quiet,
the movements evenly distributed,
the precision-controlled force.

THE REAL QUESTION: WHO DIDN'T HAVE SEX WITH THE NEANDERTHALS?

The sex rarely produced offspring but
the mixing was enough, though the love
extinct through processes of evolution,
migration via land bridges, corridors,
and horns, etc., the children looking
back at the maps which of course
were incomplete, unreliable though
200,000 years had passed. They asked,
"What about the artifacts that prove
we were here?" The broken toy, tiny
people who no longer pop up
when you push the handle. The last
awkward family photo. They can line up
the stones, pretend each one is a tool
to take them back in time. If they go,
uncover the secrets, can I even hope
they'll show me what they've found?

YOU MAKE ME FEEL
LIKE A NATURAL MUMMY

Once you die you stay
around because the climate
is dry and your grave
shallow. You're bound
to be unburied by the boy
looking for the perfect
rock to skip the tops of
waves, the mother tripping
over your shin bone
wondering what's for
dinner. They bury you
again and again with no
eulogies, no coffin parades
or casseroles, until finally
7000 years later you are
uncovered by the people
who don't believe that death
will touch them. You sit
on the beach, teeth still in
a neat row, mouth open
to tell them. All it took was
a little erosion.

JESUS HEALS A WOMAN IN THE CROWD

Detholz live at the Double Door, Chicago 2004

The plastic babies in jars must mean something
though I don't know what. The spotlight's
ordinary light might bring them to life, bass
beating out their hearts, guitars shrinking
the insides of our eyes – it's heaven again
because the music's so loud I can't
remember the thing he forgot to tell me.
He's jumping up and down in place like
the floor's a trampoline, though it doesn't
move me, the laws of physics refusing.
Even Jesus and his sad beard, his inexplicable
robe can't shake me, or won't. The babies
shudder, though they are neither happy
nor sad, neither touching nor needing
to be touched. Even if my fingers brushed
the hem of his garment he wouldn't feel it.
There are too many things to feel, too many
spaces where the love slips out and spreads
into the undulating crowd.

JESUS CLEANSES A LEPER

When the music started everyone knew
what to do but me, at the edge
of the crowd my half-shuffle wanting

to raise my hands in the air
like I just didn't care about the next
big thing, the emails and texts, those

miracle machines they say Jesus
doesn't need. When he came down
from the balcony everyone could see

his white teeth and billowing hair,
the disco pants, his boots against
the stair, and the song changed

ah-ah-ah-ah stayin' alive, stayin'
alive, the throng pulsing like a living
beast and I chose like anyone would

for him to make me clean. He stretched
out his hand, the emerald ring, and he
didn't ask why and I didn't say.

But what I wanted was to feel
the next time she broke my heart,
scratched her wicked nails across
my chest and scored the skin.

WHY HAVING A KNITTED BOYFRIEND IS BETTER THAN AN ACTUAL BOYFRIEND

For you created my inmost being; you knit me
together in my mother's womb.
Psalm 139:13

His nipples softer than expected in the dark
my face pressed into his chest after the dream

where I have once again denied my own name.
Sweat on skin, damp, sheepish, smelling

of the stripy wool socks my mother knit
for Christmas, dozens and dozens when I refused

to answer the phone. When I would not discuss
his scruff which was not scruffy, nor the speckled

line leading down from his belly button to the mystery
of his inmost being. Why is he always smiling, even

when I weep and blather awake all night? In the dream
I can only predict what has already happened –

how I drove away down the flat black road not looking
back. He was always so flat: the stuffing wouldn't last.

There were no teeth to bite the back of my neck,
no voice. No words to console, or to condemn.

SPOONING WITH KARL MARX

Karl Marx is disappearing again, beard first,
Cheshire cat style. I've grown accustomed
to the long whiskers of his chin furring

the back of my neck at night as we lie
in bed and discuss his latest theories.
This month, he's trying to travel in time

like the man in the movie we saw
at the multiplex. No one remembers, he says,
the way he used to drink wine

and sleep in late. He misses me
while he's gone but sometimes I forget to notice
the impression he's made

in the couch cushions where he'd sit
every night smoking, watching all the 24 hour
news channels simultaneously.

In the movie, the man could not control
his wanderings through time, but Karl
wants to go because no one remembers

the way he used to bring me flowers.
The way he loves me more than life, the way
he's loving everyone to death.

YOUNG JOSEPH STALIN
WOULD BANG YOUR GIRLFRIEND

He would deport you exile
you send you to correctional
labor camp and your girlfriend
would write you long letters
saying *I'm sorry I'm sorry*
he couldn't use his left arm anyway
and his face under the exquisite
mustache was scarred. In Siberia
it's too cold to hold grudges
and the thought of the naked girl
pressed under your threadbare
coat keeps you warm at night.
You might send for her but she'll
be one of the 10 million who work
and starve and in the morning
she'd have to put her clothes on
anyway. In the cold and the dark
you learn to pray to him the Father
of Nations O Brilliant Genius
of Humanity look upon your
servant. In the Old Testament
it was all sun and heat but God
sent famine too and killed everyone
he didn't like though David could
take the beautiful girl from behind
the way that makes kings feel like
men and send her husband to die in
his place. He could live and write
prayer after prayer to Him O
Gardener of Human Happiness.

SURFING THE INTERNET WITH KARL MARX

> *English sucks. Is better listen it only in russian.*
> YouTube comment, "Military Parade in
> Moscow on Victory Day, 2010"

There were 10,000 men marching
to the Kremlin, their eyes
rolled back in their heads.

On the steps, the old woman
covered her head, her hand
held out for a coin.

The men's mouths move in unison.
In the YouTube footage from 1930
the men march on without sound

in the public domain. They do not
look up at the spires of the four
churches, the golden domes.

Comments have been disabled.
They do not look the woman
in the eye. They do not sing

or shout or weep. Oh seek
and you shall find on Google all
the names of every person who shot

you in the back while your blindfold
slipped down around your collar
bone. You are the old woman,

the soldier, the indiscriminate gun,
the anonymous commenter: *only
weakling whine about governing system.*

WINSTON CHURCHILL'S PLAINLY VISIBLE DONG

He's not a young man but he stands
with his hands on his hips and looks
straight at the camera as if he knows
you will want him in you tonight
after he pulls off his Lycra suit
and leans over you making himself
harder with his own hand. Is it just
instinct to lie beneath him submitting
to the heaviness of his hip and thigh?
Perhaps it's the fact that he's winning
this war for your heart marching old men
and boys across Europe at dinner describing
the precise way your hair shines in the candle
light. Or it's the way he cries after dessert
when he's a little bit drunk for the boy
who fell before he could shoot his gun.

T.S. ELIOT BUYS ONE AND GETS ONE FREE

Because I cannot hope to discern
which brand of toilet paper is
softest against my ass, is produced
from the most recycled materials,
and is not manufactured by a boy
in Bangladesh making eleven cents
an hour. Because I cannot hope I pray
to save only money, double tuna
coupon half price Minute Rice plus
10 percent off with a store credit card.
The sign on the highway says buy one
ball get the other free and because my
children have become whores and
vipers and slaves to the $1.99 dessert
shooters at Applebees I will make
the call. I will read the fine print,
sign at the X and shave the extra
hair "down there." I will not look
the unattractive nurse in the eye
while she holds my last will and
testament in her hand before my
consciousness is severed. Because
I cannot drink for 12 hours before
the operation I will raise my glass later
for the pain, for the generations who
would paint walls white and wear
their cloaks so obviously holey though
they have the money and also weren't
cloaks on sale at Kohl's last week? I am

sorry to say that it ends here. One last
salute to the children who will not
be born. Trying to fill the cup,
thinking of the unattractive nurse,
the place where I first saw you lifting
a glass to your mouth and smiling
like you loved me or conspired to.

EMILY DICKINSON GETS A NEW LOOK

Emily, your eyes have grown deeper,
wider. When you visited the salon
for a new cut and dye job you thought
your sins would be forgiven, your central
hair cowlick made straight, the rough
places plain. But your right earlobe
is still higher than the left, your dress
still unfashionable. The white lace
at your neck itches constantly though
you pretend not to notice. The manicure
didn't last and you think perhaps plastic
surgery? A boyfriend with dark glasses
and a Mercedes, the top down. Or a new
set of dresses, each bleached white under
the sun of your father's backyard garden,
the brambles thick with thorns. The walls high.

TESTS SHOW SAINTS' SKELETAL REMAINS AT LOUISVILLE CATHOLIC CHURCH MAY BE AUTHENTIC

Saint Bonosa, St. Martin of Tours Catholic Church

The dentist has injected more
then the usual amount of Novocaine
into my lower gum because
I have been too busy defending
the faith to brush my teeth
regularly. I can speak only
through one side of my mouth,
like the devil, who I repeatedly
exhume from myself by spending
so much time on my knees
that in 1800 years the damage
will still be seen. When they open
the glass case and remove
my third century reproduction robes
they will see that I am who I said
I was. That I was 24 years old.
That I used the right hand more
than the left. What I want to know
is this: did I pray long enough to stop
the longing for the converted Roman
centurion to slip his hands under
the scratchy fabric of my dress? To shove
me against the wall before we entered
the coliseum and declared our love
of God and death?

JESUS CURSES THE FIG TREE

1000 times a day I don't believe the fig tree
withered yet the small girl woke and asked
for another piece. She grew up to hate
her mother and father who taught her
to pray to the one who made the dead
come back whether they wanted to or not,
the stink and the rot, flesh already worn
at the elbow, the knee. They showed her
how to swallow anger like bread dipped
in oil. Today it catches in her throat
with the handmade ravioli and the boyfriend
whose cock fits in her mouth like butter-
scotch biscotti, hard and soft at the same
time. Already she wishes for another piece,
giving back each word he offers, unopened.
The fig tree in the street offers one
shriveled fruit. In her mouth it plumps,
smells of the tree's memory, of the vein
of water. The sun and seed.

THE MAN WITH THE UNCLEAN SPIRIT

Jesus was 30 years old when he took the devil
out and left me limp on the shore with nothing

more to say. The waves were a record high and
the 1.2 million dollar yacht got caught fucking

the dock. I had forgotten somehow the story
I'd meant to tell, the meaning behind

the disappearing beach, though I had collected
the recommended items for my disaster supply kit:

water for drinking and sanitation, the dust
mask and moist towelettes, the battery-powered

radio that spoke but didn't listen. In the end
of the story something would drown: a dog,

the ancient fig, the herd of 2,000 pigs. Or the man
who forgot to charge his phone before turning

down the river that was once the road home.

THE FAITH OF THE ROMAN CENTURION

Today Jesus has performed 12,100,000 miracles
on Google. In .38 seconds, he has stretched out
his hand and healed at a distance the servant,
the little girl, the mother-in-law. He has warmed
my hand on the television set, through the man
who has promised healing if I confess.
Though I am paralyzed, I kneel on the hard
wood, palms against the grain, the bone-colored
sponge, making everything clean for the one
who takes possession next: my home, my heart.
Though you rolled me over in the morning
when I couldn't move, though you held my ribs
between your hands and drew my breath, still
you have gone and not returned. The phone
lies prostrate on the floor, my back against the wall,
arms not willing to lift themselves. It is a state
of being. *Helpless stoppage, inability to act.*
Have you gone to find help? To tell the Lord
I am lying at home, fearfully tormented?

COMPARABLE OBJECTS OF WORSHIP

I am making an idol from my pain, golden
and larger than life, rubbed shiny for luck

at the horn's sharp, though I have tried
to pierce myself only from the inside

because the one who breaks the silence,
the one who writes the poem without

metaphor without biblical allusion is never
forgiven. God forgave the Israelites again

and again for wanting what everyone else
had: a face to see over breakfast, the coffee

hot and mostly cream. A body in the bed.
What he gave them was a person who spoke

using only indefinite pronouns, who hid
in the sand the body of the man he killed

though he carved in stone though shalt not
kill. The pen is mightier than the sword, the Lord

thinks he knows what's best for his people;
he knows you do not need what you want.

11.

THE CLOUD WITH NO NAME

We pledge to fight "blue-sky thinking" wherever
we find it. Life would be dull if we had to look up at
cloudless monotony day after day.
Gaven Pretor-Pinney

The Cloud Appreciation Society defends
the rights of clouds to write poetry

to break up the monotony. By day the Lord
goes ahead of them in the cloud with no name,

the cloud photographed by Gaven Pretor-
Pinney who found that clouds needed

someone to say they are unjustly maligned
they are overlooked for the job, the college

education, the spot on the beach that is
just the right angle for sun borrowing

and saving. By night the Lord must change
into a pillar of fire to be seen. This might

be a message, a harbinger of some mighty
storm to come, though the cloud breaks up

over Britain to no thunderous applause.
It's not fair that no one notices, the workers

of London looking down at their phones,
the lovely words and beeps and chimes

of blue screen thinking. Their black shoes tap
tap on the sidewalk as the cloud takes

the shape of the god that held them up.
The god that sang the lullaby while they slept,

that carried their bones across the sea into
the land he had promised as their destiny.

SEGWAY OWNER DIES IN SEGWAY CRASH

It's not easy to let go and go
over the cliff in your pinstripe

suit and shiny blue tie just a few
minutes after you left church rolling

down the aisle glazed with water
from a far away sea. It's not easy

to see exactly where the land
drops off you have so much

and your glasses tint in bright
light thin and fashionable your

eyebrows rising peaks above
the wire rim. You might think it's safe

to ride across your estate on a device
of your own making but it's better

to lose control let go of the handle
bars and fly the blue sky washing

away in the river. It's a nice day
for a swim.

SEA OF GALILEE: AERIAL VIEW

From a satellite the Sea of Galilee
looks like my heart, but dark. Jesus

walked beside it one day. He said,
"come I will return the blood

to the empty space." They say dark
matter makes up most of this place,

which neither emits, nor absorbs light.
From this height the green moss around

the sea masks the fact of mostly desert.
The mountains to the east must be

my lungs. I breathe in the nothing that is
actually everything. Moss from the sea,

full of fish and leaves and other debris
might make its way to me on the jet stream

anchor itself in my esophagus. Jesus told me
to fish in this sea. Cast my net, take up

my boat, because I might bring someone
up out of the water. Someone to fill my heart

with fish and sand. Blood and bark.

A YOUNG, COOL STEPHEN HAWKING STANDING WITH HIS BRIDE

We go about our daily lives understanding
almost nothing about the world: her arms,

the black and white flowers, heavenly bodies
in the sky. This is my brief history

of happiness: someone loved me once,
though my body was already learning

the grave – the flesh, the stench
of my mouth in the morning when I spoke

of the so-called fixed stars attested to this.
In the photo leaning, I'm falling, the gravity

of the situation impossible to measure,
the lace of her dress barely brushing

my dark-suited arm, the vein of hands.

GRAVITY IS A MYSTERY

A "Let's-Read-and-Find-Out Science" book by
Franklin M. Branley

I want to lie down on the bed and press
you into me until the mattress opens

and I fall through the center of the earth,
dig the mythical hole to China, though in reality

the Indian Ocean. Down and down I would go
but never arrive at the opposite side, the earth's

center of gravity ping ponging me to itself.
In my son's book it's possible to pass

through the iron core dressed as a scientist
in hipster glasses, core marked with a red X.

No mention of impossible heat, force of two
bodies colliding layers of sand and silt, rock

and metal. Lack of air. But I don't need the breath,
just the bodies. Heat. Force of gravity pulling

everything to the center without explanation.

THE SPRINGFIELD FIRE DEPARTMENT REMINDS YOU TO BE PREPARED FOR EARTHQUAKES

Even though Vachel Lindsay drank
lye and died in this room we
make out for a few minutes when
the tour guide leaves. It's sad,
but there's a bed and we're high
on poetry and the hour long drive,
your hand resting on my thigh.
I close my eyes and see Lindsay's
visions of Old Testament prophets,
his delusions and his fears, feel
your body angled onto mine like
it was last night in the heat and
dark. The earth's moving, though not
the way it did on Feb. 28, 131 km.
south, which Lindsay may have
deemed the end of the world
if he had not already left it. At least
in this house there are no life-
sized statues of the dead and gone, as
earlier, at the museum where you slipped
your hand beneath Mary Lincoln's
ruffled skirt and twirled me into
the street under you arm. The tour guide
inevitably returns to take us back and
I pause in the doorway, practice
holding up the house as if
the shaking has not yet stopped,
as if I could know what would
happen next, and be prepared.

O THAT WITH YONDER SACRED THRONG

The things of this world do not seem
to be going according to plan.

For one thing, the altar's on fire.
The pastor hasn't noticed, thinks

the audience is unusually moved
by his words his sharp suit the way

his thick hair waves at a part
so straight the Israelites could pass

through to the Promised Land without
detour. A man in back has gone

for the fire extinguisher while
we like sheep look to one another

to gauge reaction. Shall we finish
the final hymn? Remark on the too

obvious symbolism? No, let's throw
our bodies on the flames Old Testament

style like a people uncivilized by bulletins
and keyboards and cupped ceiling lights

but living in the raw wind, the hunger.
The sand in our upturned faces.

JESUS CALMS THE STORM

Washington, IL and Union Pier, MI

When I got to the beach the storm had already arrived.
Empty bottles racing each other down the line, flat foil

of spent balloons face to face in the sand. I wanted
to send you a message, to tell you I wasn't afraid. But

the waves were turning over the abandoned toy boat.
I couldn't reach it, though I held out my hands anyway,

bringing down the anvil cloud on a string, the triangle
of wind that had already taken the city across the lake,

turned it upside down, a mirror of itself. In the last piece
of glass from the window of your mother's house

you might see me in the debris, mouth open, bending
at that angle with the garage door, holding everything

up, the sand, the water, the roof's last ridge.
Holding it all together in the wind.

WORLDOMETERS REAL-TIME WORLD STATISTICS

Early morning on the beach I am the only one
alive, though 82 million people have already

been born this year. I follow my own footsteps
to return: easier to step in the sand where I've

already been. Easier to end than to begin,
the sun bleeding even more when it rises

than when it sets. Only 35 million have died
so far this year, though I may be closer to death

than birth. The numbers change so fast it can
hardly matter. It can hardly be what you meant

when you told me you'd love me forever.
By the time I finish this poem, another 2 million

have been born, though I have not walked
on the beach again, preferring to look

from the inside out. The 7 billion people
of the world are busy loving and being loved.

The faces changing so fast it can hardly matter,
this particular you. This particular me.

BEACHED WHALE WITH SUNSET, MARCH 2012

The sunset's a 50 cent postcard but lacks
a cheesy poem to say how much we need
the clouds to spread the sun's low grace.

My son asks if a hurricane could occur.
He's obsessed with the weather, wanting
to live in the eye: state of calm with the storm

all around. We joke about apocalypse. It's 80
degrees in winter though my daughter's knees
are pale in her shorts. Tomorrow we may wake

to find a whale has beached itself on our saltless
shore. My son reminds me that a waterspout
may carry fish for miles. Why not a plague of

whales for our sin, our inability to let go?
But there's only one whale, unfurling his
intestines in the sand. My children throw

his bones like dice to reveal the past, see
the future. To find the objects they have lost:
mother, father. The waves frothing red

at the crest. Still my heart remains hard
as the children go out in the waves, out and
out, though you are no pharaoh, and I no queen.

"FAILED ICARUS"

Ron Villani 2011, acrylic on canvas

The sun has a woman's curves where his hand
caresses her: the only soft place. On his body
the obvious ribs, his other hand a fist.
He leans in. For a kiss? His shape suggests
something more. But the heat
might be too much – opens his mouth, turns
his clenched teeth red. In the myth, he falls
before he reaches her. Drowns. His defeat sure.
But here the dark water's distant. Perhaps
another kind of hell, lacking a cool end.
Instead, one black tear from his melting face,
the flesh gray. Red. Still he won't
give up. *I've left everything for you.* My heart.
The ground. The home I once knew.

ASTRONOMY PICTURE OF THE DAY:
STILL LIFE WITH REFLECTING DUST

You could lose yourself in the tangle
of my hair but for the blue

stars shining through, though you can't
love me the way you wanted to –

the heat, the reds and blues, canvas
15 light years across. You can't

love me though I'm impressively close
if you look this way on the screen

a slice of cosmos thin as paper, thin
as my voice on the phone today

four hours away and nothing
more I can say.

EVENT HORIZON WITH SUNSET

$$d_p = \int_0^{t_0} \frac{c}{a(t)} \, dt.$$

Even if I were to emit light
it would never reach you: point
of no return. I have absorbed

all stars and minor suns
of this galaxy which may be
too remote for the telescope's

notice. When you approach
the place where sky meets sea
you appear to slow down never

quite passing through, your shape
silver shift in the sand. All light-
like paths have arced into

the sun falling into itself. It's possible
for any matter to become a black
hole if compressed enough, the earth

squeezed to a 9 millimeter smudge,
all of us undetectable to the rest
of the universe, no matter where

the telescopes point. No matter
who's looking.

THE CLOCK OF THE LONG NOW

In 10,000 years my bones may still show
the shape I had when you walked up to me
in the bar and couldn't stop looking.

If the soil is of neutral acidity the evolved
people of the future may put me back
together and give me a name that is not

mine. In acid peaty soil my bones would
dissolve before you could text me the next
morning and ask what it was that I wanted.

What was it? In the graveyard my son
presses his fingers to the place where
the name carved in stone can no longer

be read. Who is it? he says. Who is it?

YAHOO ANSWERS: "HOW LONG DOES IT TAKE FOR A HUMAN BODY TO COMPLETELY DECOMPOSE AFTER IT'S BEEN EMBALMED?"

When your heart stops pumping
blood the skin does not stop
feeling the lover's last tooth,
sharp at the back of the neck,
for 24 hours. How romantic the rain,
how warm the soil under sun
where the flesh liquefies in less
time than it took for you to say
I love you. The tooth may last
for hundreds of years, being bone
but harder, and for 3 to 7 minutes
the brain remembers uncountable
stars, the multiplication facts
from third grade, the constellation
of freckles above my right thigh.
The farther underground the longer
you may last. What is it, if not
a place to hide from you sins? From
the swell and the stink, skin blueing
the body eating itself. Even there
he will find you, making your bed
in the depths. And this is supposed
to be your comfort, your place of rest?

111.

THE SPRINGFIELD FIRE DEPARTMENT OFFERS TURKEY FRYER SAFETY TIPS

It's not enough to bathe the body
in salt, to place in the space

between rib and backbone the bread
and the sage, to slide the pan

in the oven and wait the span
of a 1,000 piece jigsaw puzzle.

The fryer is faster though the fat
may spatter grandmother's 73

year old hand sewn apron and
catch fire. Keep an extinguisher

nearby. Do not douse with water;
cover and let the flame burn down

to the bone, the crackling skin.
Pay close attention. It is not enough

to add butter and longing every hour.
Instead, you must lower the body

slowly, away from the house. Sing
your song and move on.

COMPLETE INSTRUCTIONS FOR PLAYING AMAZING GRACE ON THE BAGPIPE

When you came up
out of your office into
the customary light you

heard it. In the gap
between the two
buildings you heard

it bounce one to the
other. You on one
side with your red

ball cap the priest
on the other wearing
purple the veil of

light cloud 57 degrees
and high humidity.
You heard it and

the air lifted just
a slender wing flap
of skin paper cut

blood turning blue
to red. This is not
a cliché because you

are the one who
turned his head
who broke the barrier

between sound and
the desire to say
that it matters.

You the particular one
stopping to listen
to rub between your

thumb and forefinger
the sweat of sky on brick.

I TAKE A SURREAL MORNING WALK
WITH MARY OLIVER

I hadn't dressed suitably for the seagull convention:
they in their white lab coats, me in my red jacket
and exercise pants. Perhaps that explained why they wouldn't
let me listen to the lecture on the beach—moved
to the ballroom which was larger anyway, and blue.

Morning was coming up opposite, turning sky over water.
The birds moved to the back row so I couldn't hear
their cackles at the speaker's jokes—just a mechanical
sound from a house on the dune and the waves
measuring with a regular woosh my embarrassment
at choice of dress. My vulgar lack of wing.

THE PARABLE OF THE GREAT BANQUET

I have bought 5 yoke
of oxen to mow the unruly
hair of the dead body
out back where the vultures
gather: leaves from last
year's disappointment,
the stumps that refuse
digging and flogging and all
other forms of affection.
If I put my arms around
the tallest oak and kiss
the dark root, eat the splinter
bark that splits the tongue.
If I lie down in the field
and turn my eye to branch
and sky. Oh taste and see
that the tree is good and lives
deeper beneath than above,
grows like a secret in the dark.

DESK, WITH WINDOW FRAME AND HEAVEN

Only the tops of trees, the blue sky.
Sometimes a bird passing by. No sound

from outside; the window won't open.
You ask me where I am. What I see.

Sometimes all I see are the words behind
my eyes. Sometimes, a book on the desk:

Life of the Beloved. The Long Home. Or,
a single sheet with that poem about

falling in love. And there's Jesus above
on the cross, looking sad. We are all sad,

aren't we? Sometimes the white clouds
billowing up. The flock of birds that

sing so loud I let them in.

MUSIC OF THE SPHERES:
SIX UNACCOMPANIED CELLO SUITES
[DISC 2]

I'm trying to tell you
what I hear, listening to Bach
in the dark, moon waiting to

rise above the barn next
door, my mind the earth
circling itself. On the stereo

the cello sounds like two
voices, though it plays alone.
It's a kind of silence and in

the silence I'm trying to hear
the music Pythagoras said
the planets might be—a sacred

geometry. I want to take this into me,
see the spaces between stars where
the voices resonate. This is the way

sound arrives, the way these parallel
strings kiss the air, your arm
bent across the body with the bow.

A CONFESSION

based on the Holy Eucharist Rite Two Confession,
The Book of Common Prayer, 1979

I confess that I have held
against you my very body the one
that I love at times, and at others hate

in thought, word, and deed,
and I know what I have done has not
broken you, but what I have left

undone. I confess I have not
loved you with my whole heart;
I have not loved you as I love

myself this dusty house, those rooms
I have locked away without
remembering why. I have not

loved. I have not loved. This
is a plea for your grace, your mercy
that is not a mist in the air,

nor a cloud of scent. It is for your body
with mine again, the hard places
and the soft. The delight. The
glory and the flame.

THIS MORNING IN CHURCH: AN INVOCATION TO THE MUSE

Words on the tongue might be magic, might bring
the god again. He came once but didn't stay. If we
say the words this way. If we sing the song thus:
ask the god to dwell among within us. Between the
words. Silence on the lips, the flesh the blood—you
said sweetness tastes on the tip of the tongue. I hold
the bread there, remember the taste of your mouth
on mine dear God, bring me a poem. Bring me the
tongues not of angels but of man, this man. The one
who dwells among within my body here, the sheets
wild with prayer.

IF I CAN'T KISS YOU, I MIGHT AS WELL WRITE A POEM

After watching the made-for-TV Oprah movie Their
Eyes Were Watching God

You are driving in the dark on your way
to make paragraphs from a mess of words,
and I sit at home Googling Oprah,

because Oprah wants to be kissed like that –
two tongues touching mouths open eyes
open tongue against cheek against lip –

which made the girls in back laugh.
The Internet is a mess of words.
Oprah's boyfriend stole from her.

He made her smoke crack. He won't
marry her. You are driving in the dark,
your lips open on a $1.69 hamburger,

subconsciously demonstrating our last
kiss. I am making my own paragraph
from these words. Dear Oprah, Dear

Giggling Girls, how to explain the shape
of his lips, his tongue making the words
your mouth will form. How his breath
becomes your own.

TAKE THE PLANK OUT OF YOUR OWN EYE

Yes I do come here often and
yes I do talk to myself in
the grocery store when trying
to decide on baked chips are

they really healthier? Listen
I am talking to you, me,
do you think you can continue
down the aisle with your big

ass cart and ignore the aliens
using the self-check out line?
They of course have huge heads
in relation to their bodies and

wrinkly gray skin just like they
should and there's an eerie blue
light advertising a special on my
right breast and suddenly I am

writing a poem not about my
own blindness but about the
way you hold me and won't
let go even when the blue light

comes in through the blinds in
the morning and it's time to go.

POETS WITHOUT CLOTHES

Poet, intergalactic traveler,
Allen Ginsberg with your plastic
cup of wine, still life
or portrait my darling
my dear it's divine to have this
some of the time, though I'm cold
in the vulnerable air. Warm me
with your breath, your book,
placed strategically at the
point around which your soul
revolves. Stand up, don't be
afraid to speak directly
into the mic to the audience,
naked and trying to be
unashamed. Form the words
with your own two lips,
your belly and thigh, your
mouth on mine sing
your hymn. You know I want
you to fly.

ACCIDENTAL PORN

The poetry slam promises public
demonstrations of crying, doppelganger
forms, and lines that reveal

what we long for: x, x, x, solving
for the unknown, or sometimes LIVE
NUDE GIRLS. The boy who wants

to lie down in the fountain and sing
to Demeter wears a crutch and is
slow to take his prize. The girl

whose sitter shook her as an infant
has risen from her bed. Her horse
has wings, though she sometimes

fears him. Tomorrow, Jesus will lie
in the tomb with them, the fountain
the bed, his long fingers folded over

one another. Two coins on his eyes.
He has taken first prize, but always
wants to share, unlike us. His example

impossible to live up to. But
blessed are we anyway: the poor
in spirit. The ones who mourn.

JESUS ACCELERATES A PARTICLE

Because of its success in explaining a wide variety of exper-
imental results, the Standard Model is sometimes regarded
as a "theory of almost everything."
Wikipedia

96% of the universe is what we don't
see. When Jesus held up his arms

to part the atoms he did not indicate
you had to have mass: your particles

all accounted for but the one that really
mattered. He did not specify you the one

to live forever, the one to write the poem
that completes the theory of everything.

It is not possible to see in the dark to
discover the spot on the x-ray where expansion

of the universe is apparent. He, who put
you together in, who knew you when, raising

his arms, letting you go, accelerating you
toward the speed of light though you never

quite arrive. Your body gaining mass your
hair growing back, time slowing down

for everyone but you.

NOTES

"Complete Instructions for Playing Amazing Grace on the Bagpipe" is for Thom Caraway.

"Jesus Accelerates a Particle" is for Chris Wiman

Thanks especially to David Wright, Tania Runyan, Sarah Wells, and Dave Harrity, for their close readings and editorial insights.

Several poems were inspired by or refer to web content, found at the following sites:

i.
Mr. Rogers is Flipping You Off:
    http://www.cracked.com/blog/14-photo-graphs-that-shatter-your-image-famous-people/

Apparatus for Facilitating the Birth of a Child by Centrifugal Force:
    https://dublin.sciencegallery.com/failbetter/apparatusfacilitatingbirthchildcentrifugalforce

The Real Question: Who Didn't Have Sex With the Neanderthals?:
    http://news.yahoo.com/real-didnt-sex-neander-thals-134026418.html

You Make Me Feel Like a Natural Mummy:
http://www.npr.org/2012/08/15/158790969/
changing-climate-may-have-led-to-earliest-
mummies?utm_source=npr&utm_medium=-
facebook&utm_campaign=20120815

Why Having a Knitted Boyfriend Is Better Than an
Actual Boyfriend:
http://www.buzzfeed.com/alannaokun/why-
having-a-knitted-boyfriend-is-better-than-an-
actual-boyf

Young Joseph Stalin Would Bang Your Girlfriend:
http://www.cracked.com/blog/14-photo-
graphs-that-shatter-your-image-famous-people/

Winston Churchill's Plainly Visible Dong:
http://www.cracked.com/blog/14-photo-
graphs-that-shatter-your-image-famous-peo-
ple_p2/

Emily Dickinson Gets a New Look:
http://www.guardian.co.uk/books/2012/
sep/05/emily-dickinson-new-photograph

Tests Show Saints' Skeletal Remains at Louisville
Catholic Church May Be Authentic:
http://www.courier-journal.com/arti-
cle/20120923/NEWS01/309230067/
Tests-show-saints-skeletal-remains-Louis-
ville-Catholic-church-may-authentic

ii.
The Cloud with No Name:
   http://www.dailymail.co.uk/sciencetech/
   article-1189877/The-cloud-Meteorolo-
   gists-campaign-classify-unique-Aspera-
   tus-clouds-seen-world.html

Segway Owner Dies in Segway Crash:
   http://wheels.blogs.nytimes.com/2010/09/27/
   segway-owner-dies-in-segway-crash/

Sea of Galilee: Aerial View:
   http://www.aerialviews.org/map/Sea_of_Gal-
   ilee

A Young, Cool Stephen Hawking Standing With
His Bride:
   http://www.cracked.com/blog/14-photo-
   graphs-that-shatter-your-image-famous-people/

The Springfield Fire Department Reminds You to
Be Prepared for Earthquakes:
   http://www.springfield.il.us/

Worldometers Real-Time World Statistics:
   http://www.worldometers.info/

Astronomy Picture of the Day: Still Life with Re-
flecting Dust:
   http://apod.nasa.gov/apod/ap130707.html

Event Horizon with Sunset:
   http://en.wikipedia.org/wiki/Event_horizon

The Clock of the Long Now:
    http://spectrum.ieee.org/geek-life/profiles/en-
    gineering-the-10-000year-clock/0

Yahoo Answers: "How long does it take for a hu-
man body to completely decompose after it's been
embalmed?":
    http://answers.yahoo.com/question/index-
    ?qid=20070804095320AAabFgu

iii.
The Springfield Fire Department Offers Turkey
Fryer Safety Tips:
    http://www.springfield.il.us/

Poets without Clothes:
    http://poetswithoutclothes.tumblr.com/

ACKNOWLEDGEMENTS

Thanks to the editors of the following journals in which these poems, some under other titles or in different versions, have appeared:

491 Magazine, "I Take a Surreal Walk with Mary Oliver"

Books & Culture, "Jesus Accelerates a Particle," "Segway Owner Dies in Segway Crash"

The Christian Century, "Sea of Galilee: Aerial View"

The Collagist, "Mr. Rogers Is Flipping You Off"

The Curator, "The Parable of the Great Banquet"

Everyday Poems, "Gravity Is a Mystery"

Hobart, "The Springfield Fire Department Offers Turkey Fryer Safety Tips," "The Springfield Fire Department Reminds You to Be Prepared for Earthquakes," "Tests Show Saints' Skeletal Remains at Louisville Catholic Church May Be Authentic," "The Faith of the Roman Centurion," "Jesus Heals a Woman in the Crowd"

The Louisville Review, "Failed Icarus"

Metazen, "Take the Plank Out of Your Own Eye"

The Other Journal, "Desk with Window Frame and Heaven"

Perspectives, "Conversion: Complete Instructions for Playing Amazing Grace on the Bagpipe"

Quiddity, "Worldometers Real Time World Statistics," "The Clock of the Long Now"

Redivider, "T.S. Eliot Buys One and Gets One Free"

Relief, "Music of the Spheres: Six Unaccompanied Cello Suites [Disc 2]"

Rock & Sling, "O That With Yonder Sacred Throng," "This Morning in Church"

St. Katherine Review, "Accidental Porn"

Windhover, "Comparable Objects of Worship"

"Oh That With Yonder Sacred Throng" also appeared in the anthology, *Light Upon Light: A Literary Guide to Prayer for Advent, Christmas, and Epiphany* (Paraclete Press)

ABOUT THE AUTHOR

Marci Rae Johnson teaches English at Purdue University
North Central. She is also the poetry editor for Word-
Farm press. Her poems appear in *The Collagist, Quiddity,
Hobart, Redivider, Redactions, The Valparaiso Poetry Re-
view, The Louisville Review,* and *32 Poems,* among others.
Her first collection of poetry, *The Eyes the Window,* won
the Powder Horn Prize and was published by Sage Hill
Press in 2013, and her poetry chapbook won the Friends
of Poetry chapbook contest for Michigan authors in 2014
and was published by Celery City Chapbooks.

CPSIA information can be obtained at www.ICGtesting.com
Printed in the USA
BVOW06s1633311215

431309BV00020BA/306/P

9 780986 357510